HOW TO RECEIVE **GOD'S EXTRAVAGANT GENEROSITY**

HOW TO RECEIVE GOD'S EXTRAVAGANT GENEROSITY

Mark & Trina Hankins

How to Receive God's Extravagant Generosity
ISBN # 978-1-889981-58-1

First Edition 2018

Published By
MHM Publications
P.O. Box 12863
Alexandria, LA 71315
www.markhankins.org

Printed in the United States of America.

TABLE OF CONTENTS

❝ Like a mother *smiles* her baby into *smiling*, God *loves* us into *loving* & He *gives* us into *giving*.

Mark Hankins

1

HOW TO RECEIVE GOD'S EXTRAVAGENT GENEROSITY

Proverbs 11:24 (Message) says, *"The world of the generous gets larger and larger...."* This book is about generosity in the area of finances and giving. In studying this subject in the Bible, you will find there are over 2,000 scriptures on finances. In comparison, there are about 500 scriptures mentioning the word faith and another 500 that mention the word prayer. Of course faith and prayer are very important, yet there are more than four times as many scriptures referring to finances.

Generosity is very important to God. It is one of His most outstanding characteristics. As a matter of fact, God Himself is extravagantly generous in every area. For example, the Bible says God is rich in mercy (Ephesians 2:4); so rich that His mercies are new every morning (Lamentations 3:22-23). He also overflows in grace. His grace is abundant, far exceeding our sin and any evil thing that has ever happened to us.

I once heard someone say, "A mother can smile her baby into smiling." Is that not one of the most beautiful things—to see a mother smiling and her baby smiling back? It is the same with God, **"Like a mother smiles her baby into smiling, God loves us into loving and He gives us into giving."** Our personal generosity is a demonstration of our understanding and revelation of God's generosity toward us.

66 Most people
give with a
consciousness
of *their giving*
rather than a
consciousness
of *God's
generosity*.

Mark Hankins

2

PLEADING A CASE
ON THE BASIS OF
GENEROSITY

Rev. Kenneth E. Hagin (Dad Hagin) came to my dad's church when I was 17 and told about a leader in his church who gave 30 percent of his income. This man had an accident at work and was about to die. The doctor said, "He cannot live and if he does, he will be a cripple all of his life."

Dad Hagin went to the hospital to pray for this man and state his case to God. He said, "Lord, I cannot let him die. He serves in the church. He is very valuable and important in the community. He gives 30 percent of his income to the church. Lord, I need him. If I need him, You need him. I will not let him die. I cannot let him die, I need him here." Dad Hagin said he prayed this way all night long.

The man recovered and was perfectly healed. Later, the man told Dad Hagin that he had been in Heaven. Jesus pulled back the curtain and said, "Your pastor will not let you die." Isn't that interesting? It seems this man's service and generosity enabled his pastor to plead his case before God.

66 You can tithe
on what
you make
or on what
*you want
to make.*

Pastor B.B. Hankins

3

MY TESTIMONY OF GOD'S FAITHFULNESS

My parents were 50 percent givers, and always taught us to tithe. My dad would actually figure it for us. When I was a child, I might get three dollars for mowing the yard and he would say, "Now remember to honor God first." Then, as a teenager, I started double-tithing (which is really tithing and sowing) by giving 20 percent.

When I heard Dad Hagin tell the story about the man who gave 30 percent, I was just a teenager. I decided I was going to do that. I did not do it right away, but I purposed in my heart to get to that level.

When Trina and I met and talked about getting married, I was very honest with her. I told her about my financial covenant with God and that I was a 20 percent giver. In those days I made $100 a week. Trina and I had no furniture when we were first married. Everything we owned fit in my car when we were first married.

My grandma had died and left her furniture to my dad. My daddy was very generous with God, but when it came to us kids, he said, "There is a God and I am not Him." Do you know what that means? He was saying, "You need to get a job and use your own faith in God!"

When I asked my dad about using the furniture, he said he would set up a payment plan for me. It almost made me mad! But then I thought, "There is a God, and my daddy is not the source of my supply. God is my source!" So my daddy actually taught me how to have faith in God.

Even though we did not have much, Trina and I began our marriage as 20 percent givers. I told her before we married that she might not have the fanciest furniture or nicest car right away, but in time she would.

Over the next few years, both of our children were born. When they came along, I was pastoring a church and making $160 a week. The Lord spoke to me and said, "When would you like to increase to that 30 percent you said you wanted to do?" I said, "Well, Lord, not right now! Obviously, this is not a good time. I have two kids and no insurance. It is not a good time for generosity."

Around that time, I read Malachi 3 where it says your tithes and offerings open the windows of Heaven. Verse 10 says, **"Prove me now."** Those three words jumped off the page and hit me. I went to Trina and said, "I have always wanted to do this. Let's crank it up to 30 percent." She said, "Good! Let's do it!"

We increased our giving to 30 percent, and my hands literally broke out in a sweat every Sunday when I wrote my offering check. But I remembered that God said He would multiply our seed, so I stayed faithful.

That was years ago and our 30 percent was about $50 a week. I noticed that $50 a week turned into $100 a week, then $200 a week, then $300, then $500, then $1,000, then $2,000, and on to $10,000 a week!

There are no limits to this! Now, to be clear, I am not talking about some get rich quick scheme. I am talking about a 40 year story of giving and receiving. **My dad always told me, "You can tithe on what you make or on what you want to make."** Psalm 24:1 says, *"The earth is the Lord's and the fullness thereof."* Your generosity will unlock God's ability and His generosity.

FROM GENERATION TO GENERATION

When you give to the Kingdom of God, your generosity affects future generations. My grandfather was the first in the Hankins family to be born again, filled with the Holy Spirit, and called to preach the Gospel. By most standards, my grandfather was very poor, but he did not let that stop him from pioneering many churches in east Texas.

In those days, people did not have a lot of money for tithes and offerings. Instead, they brought chickens, milk, eggs, or vegetables from their gardens to their pastor as tithes and offerings. I will never forget a story I heard my daddy tell about my grandfather. His car had broken down and he had to walk everywhere. He would walk into town and knock on doors, ministering to people and preaching the Gospel.

He could not get a loan from the bank so he started saving up money to buy a car. Over time, he saved up about two or three hundred dollars. A missionary from Africa came to preach at his church. My grandpa was so touched by the missionary and his work, that he took the money he had saved up for the car and gave it all to missions.

When my grandma found out, she was very upset. She would not talk to my grandpa for days. She said, "We have no transportation but you took all the money we have been saving for a car and gave it to a missionary." Not only was she frustrated, but the kids were too! Thankfully, the story does not end there. My dad told us how just a few weeks later, someone gave my grandpa a better car than he ever could have bought with his savings!

The greatest part of this story is that my grandfather loved preaching the Gospel and he loved world missions. He never preached outside of the state of Texas, but his generosity opened the door for me, his grandson, to preach all over the world. I am not preaching around the world today just because of what I have done. I am walking through doors my grandpa—and even my father—opened for me with their generosity.

It is a Bible promise that your generosity will affect your children and your grandchildren. Even after your funeral, your generosity will still be speaking. It will be a blessing for generations to come (Psalm 112:1-3; 115:14).

66 Your giving *reflects* your heart, it also *affects* your heart.

Mark Hankins

4

INSTRUCTIONS FOR
RICH PEOPLE

*Charge them that are rich in this world, that
they be not high-minded, nor trust in uncertain
riches, but in the living God, who giveth us richly
all things to enjoy. That they do good, that
they be rich in good works, ready to distribute,
willing to communicate; Laying up in store for
themselves a good foundation against the time
to come, that they may lay hold on eternal life.
-1 Timothy 6:17-19*

Paul gave specific instructions to Timothy
(who was a pastor) to talk to the rich people about

generosity. When I read that, I realized there are supposed to be rich people at church. Otherwise, the Bible would not say to talk to them. So, I volunteered for the program!

Before we go any further, let's define what "rich" really means. Some people may think they do not fit in that economic category. They think the word "rich" applies only to people like Donald Trump, Bill Gates, or Warren Buffett. Actually, if you make $35,000 or more a year you are in the top four percent of the richest people in the world. In other words, you have more money than 96 percent of people in the world. The majority of Americans could be considered extremely rich compared to most of the world.

Let's now go back to what Paul told Timothy. He basically said, "Listen, Timothy. You need to talk to the rich people, because with abundance comes responsibility. Tell those who are rich in this world not to be high-minded." In other words, having money does not make you more valuable. The blood of Jesus was shed for everyone, both rich and poor.

Oftentimes, we need to deal with our attitude, especially if we have an abundance. This passage warns us not to be high-minded or trust in uncertain riches. It is okay to have money, but do not put your trust in it. Having faith in God is much greater than having money. Money makes a very poor god, so be sure you trust in the living God Who gives you richly all things to enjoy (1 Timothy 6:17).

God is not opposed to people being rich, but He is opposed to people being covetous. In Matthew 6:21, Jesus said, *"For where your treasure is, there will your heart be also."* Your generosity is a reflection of your heart. I heard Billy Graham say, "Show me your checkbook and I will show you what you value." In other words, what you spend your money on is what you value.

Some people value their cars, their clothes, their hair, their hunting rifles, and many other things more than they value the work of God. Generosity is not a minor subject with Jesus or a minor subject in the Bible because it reveals the condition of your heart. **Your giving reflects your heart, it also affects your heart.**

In 1 Timothy 6:17 (Message) it says, *"Tell the rich people to be extravagantly generous."* Remember, you are probably the rich person he was talking to, so do not put this off on somebody who makes more money than you. Some people try to say they are just frugal. It is okay to be frugal, but do not be frugal with God. When it comes to the work of God, the gospel of Jesus, and helping others, we need to be generous!

What is a good definition for "extravagantly generous?" It means to be excessive, excessively generous, unrestrained, lavish, overboard, limitless, or superabundant. I call it **"extreme generosity."**

EXTREME GENEROSITY

You might know people who are into extreme sports. They like to jump off mountains with wings, flip motorcycles, and bungee jump off bridges. They love the risk and the thrill they get. I say these things are not extreme. If you really want to get some excitement or a thrill, try giving 50 percent of your income for the rest of your life! That will really give you a thrill. When you enter into extreme generosity, you better know there is a God and that He will multiply your seed sown.

Here is the way the Lord said it to me: **"Your extravagant generosity is a reflection of God's extravagant generosity."** This extravagant generosity takes you beyond your comfort zone to a place where your faith is in God alone. This is when God becomes the source of your supply.

Did you know that God wants to bless you and enable you to give beyond your wildest dreams? **You can give more than you have ever given and still have more than you have ever had.**

Someone might wonder how that is possible. It is simple. As you give, you put God's law of sowing and reaping into operation. And you will see a return on your seed sown. **God is not planning on you giving yourself broke!** He gives seed to the sower. Isaiah 32:8 (NKJV) says, *"But a generous man devises generous things, and by generosity he shall stand."* God ensures that the sower has a full supply.

The woman in Mark 14 was extravagant in her lavish outpouring of the perfumed ointment on Jesus' head. The alabaster box typically cost a year's wages. Some around her were indignant and called it wasteful. They said it could have been sold and the money given to the poor. But notice how Jesus responded. He said, "Put that on me. You will always have the poor, but you will not always have me."

Jesus said in Mark 14:9, *"Verily I say unto you, Wheresoever this gospel shall be preached throughout the whole world, this also that she hath done shall be spoken of for a memorial of her."* This woman's act of honor—her extravagant generosity—propelled Jesus to His destiny and comforted Him all the way to the cross. You see, while many were spitting on and cursing Him, Jesus could still smell the aroma of that perfume. This woman helped Jesus fulfill His destiny. What a legacy!

I also want you to notice how this woman worshipped with her giving, even though she did not sing any songs. Likewise, your giving is a significant part of your worship of God.

Your extravagant generosity will be a memorial to you, just as her giving was to her. God does not want you to hold back in generosity, but to enter into extreme generosity.

66 With God,
payday isn't
always on Friday,
or the first, or
the fifteenth, but
God's paydays
always come!

Pastor B.B. Hankins

5

GOD'S PAYDAYS
ALWAYS COME

Giving gets God's attention. He is impressed with generosity and remembers it.

> *For God is not unrighteous to forget your work*
> *and labour of love, which ye have shewed*
> *toward his name, in that ye have ministered to*
> *the saints, and do minister.*
> *-Hebrews 6:10*

God does not have a memory problem. People may forget how you served, what you did, and how you gave, but God never forgets! My dad used to say, "With God, payday is not always on Friday, or the 'first' or the 'fifteenth,' but God's paydays always come." Ruth 2:12 says, *"The Lord recompense thy work, and a full reward be given thee of the Lord God of Israel, under whose wings thou art come to trust."* Hebrews 10:35 also mentions your reward: *"Cast not away therefore your confidence, which hath great recompense of reward."*

The harvest you are believing for may not come every Friday, but God says, I have not forgotten. There is a harvest of blessing that will come to you at the most unusual time and it will come in many different ways. **The seed is guaranteed! It has a return address. Your harvest never gets confused!**

66 God loves
everybody,
but He
gives *special*
attention to
generous
givers.

Mark Hankins

6

GENEROSITY GETS GOD'S ATTENTION

One of my favorite stories about generosity is in Acts 10. This chapter tells us about Cornelius who was a rich man. The Bible says his prayers and his giving came up before God regularly. Cornelius was not even a Christian. He loved God, but he did not know the Lord Jesus. However, the Bible says his generosity got God's attention.

If the Lord pays attention to the non-Christian's giving, I know He pays attention to His children's giving. As a matter of fact, Jesus watched as people gave their offerings and He made comments.

Jesus sat down near the collection box in the Temple and watched as the crowds dropped in their money. Many rich people put in large amounts. Then a poor widow came and dropped in two small coins. Jesus called his disciples to him and said, "I tell you the truth, this poor widow has given more than all the others who are making contributions. For they gave a tiny part of their surplus, but she, poor as she is, has given everything she had to live on.

-Mark 12:41-44 (NLT)

The fascinating thing about Jesus watching what people are giving is, He knows how much money they have left. It is not about equal gifts but *equal sacrifice.*

Some of the rich people were probably putting in large amounts of money, but Jesus noticed there was a certain woman who gave of her living. In other words, even though she had less financial ability than the rich people, in Jesus' eyes she was the most generous person there. God loves everybody, but He gives special attention to generous givers.

Since Jesus never changes (Hebrews 13:8), I believe He still watches and makes comments today. You do not have to be a rich person to be generous. Anyone can qualify for generosity. I am not just talking about a certain economical class of people. You do not have to be a rich person to get God's attention with your generosity. Being generous is different amounts to different people. That means it is possible to be more generous than people who have more money than you do.

66 When you're a *generous giver*, God does things for you that *money cannot do.*

Mark Hankins

7

TRUE RICHES

He who is faithful in what is least is faithful
also in much; and he who is unjust in what
is least is unjust also in much. Therefore, if
you have not been faithful in the unrighteous
mammon, who will commit to your trust the
true riches?
-Luke 16:10-11

In Luke 16, Jesus said, *"If you are faithful in the*
area of money, God will commit to you true riches." In other
words, money is not true riches. True riches are things
that are much better than money—such as wisdom,

revelation knowledge, a friend when you need a friend, opportunities, the goodness of God, health, and your family. These are things no amount of money can buy. **When you are a generous giver, God does things for you that money cannot do!**

I have a minister friend who worked for Kenneth Hagin Ministries for many years. One day he asked Dad Hagin, "What is the number one characteristic you look for in a leader?" Without hesitation, Dad Hagin responded, "generosity." He added, "a person who is not generous will shut down the move of God." That is interesting because of all the qualities Dad Hagin could have mentioned, generosity was the most important.

In studying the Bible, you will find there are several outstanding verses about generosity. One of my favorites is found in 1 Chronicles 29, which talks about the generosity of David. Really, it is not just an isolated verse here but an entire chapter devoted to the subject of David's generosity.

It was time to build the house of God and David said in 1 Chronicles 29:2a, 3, *"Now I have prepared with all my might for the house of my God...because I have set my affection to the house of my God, I have of mine own proper good, of gold and silver, which I have given to the house of my God, over and above all that I have prepared for the holy house."* The New English Bible in verse 3 says, *"Further, because I delight in the house of my God, I give of my own private store of gold and silver for the house of my God – over and above all the store which I have collected for the sanctuary."* Notice the phrase "over and above" in this verse. The Lord said it to me this way: **"Over and above giving will produce over and above living!"** Glory to God!

Returning to the story, I want you to notice that David declared how much he planned to give. I heard someone say David was the first declared steward in the Bible, meaning he told how much he gave. Today, his giving would have amounted to around 1.5 billion dollars. Wow!

Now, in those days, you could not write a check. So David brought wagons and wagons filled with gold and silver for the house of God. Not only that, but he then turned to his mighty men and said, *"And who then is willing to consecrate his service this day unto the Lord?"* (1 Chronicles 29:5b). David asked his guys what they were willing to do in the area of their giving.

Many today would have answered that with, "I just want to sing in the choir!" **A lot of people want to sing like David sang, or dance like David danced. But there are just not too many people who want to give like David gave!** You could say David's singing and dancing were a reflection of his generosity. He was so free to worship, because he knew God was the source of his supply. When David gave to the work of God, he understood his generosity would affect future generations. And it did! His generosity blessed the next generation and the one after that. He was known as a man after God's own heart. His heart was reflected in his generosity to the work of God.

Remember those mighty men—the same men who had come to him distressed, discontented, and in debt (1 Samuel 22:2). They gave over 2.5 billion dollars (in today's dollars). David had 400 mighty men and each one gave millions of dollars! Apparently, they got out of debt!

It is interesting to note that "distressed, discontented, and in debt" people usually hang out together. Your life may have started out that way but it doesn't have to stay that way. Your covenant with God can radically change your whole life. As those men spent time with David, they caught the same spirit of faith he had. They learned to love the presence of God. And together with David, these mighty men gave and rejoiced with exceedingly great joy. In 1 Chronicles 29:18, David said, *"Lord, keep this forever in the imagination of the thoughts of the hearts of the people."* He said in verse 14, *"But who am I...that we should be able to offer so willingly?"*

Just like David, the giving of these men was a reflection of their affection for God. As you catch the spirit of faith and grow in revelation knowledge, your generosity will also be a reflection of God's generosity.

66 God's
sowing system
will always
outperform man's
saving system!

Mark Hankins

8

GOD LOVES A CHEERFUL GIVER

Every man according as he purposeth in his heart, so let him give; not grudgingly, or of necessity: for God loveth a cheerful giver.
-2 Corinthians 9:7

For God loves the hilarious giver (the laughing giver).
-Godbey

God loves, (He takes pleasure in, prizes above other things, and is not willing to abandon or

> *do without) a cheerful, (joyous, "prompt to do*
> *it") giver [whose heart is in his giving.]*
> *-2 Corinthians 9:7 (AMP)*

In over 25 years of pastoring, I found that the quietest part of the service was when it was time to receive the tithes and offerings. However, all through the scriptures I found people who were extremely happy about giving. I asked the Lord, "Why do my people not get happier when it is time to tithe and give?" The Lord answered, "Most people give just enough to irritate themselves." Most people give with a consciousness of *their* giving rather than a consciousness of *God's* generosity.

You see, some people give and think **subtraction**. They feel a sense of loss. However, God says, "I will **multiply** your seed sown!" Therefore, you should give with an expectation of increase and provision in mind. You should give with the promises of God in mind. The Lord said to me, "You can give your way into abundance."

*There is that scattereth, and yet increaseth; and
there is that withholdeth more than is meet, but
it tendeth to poverty. The liberal soul shall be
made fat: and he that watereth shall be watered
also himself.*
-Proverbs 11:24-25

*One gives away, and still he grows the richer:
another keeps what he should give, and is the
poorer. A liberal soul will be enriched, and he
who waters will himself be watered.*
-Moffat

The Bible promises the generous person will be abundantly provided for. The key word here is **generous**. You see, this scripture does not say that someone did not give. It says they withheld more than is appropriate, meaning they were not generous.

I studied this scripture for years and finally said, "Lord, I really do not understand this. What are you trying to say?" This is how He explained it to me: "You would think that if you withhold money, you would have **more** money. But if you hold on too tightly, you will have **less** money." In 2 Corinthians

9:6 it says, *"But this I say, He which soweth sparingly shall reap also sparingly; and he which soweth bountifully shall reap also bountifully."* Lack does not come from money you do not have. It comes from money you do have that you should not have. God's sowing system will always outperform man's saving system!

> *Not, how much of my money will I give to God, but, how much of God's money will I keep for myself?*
> *- John Wesley*

> *No one has ever become poor by giving.*
> *- Anne Frank*

Your generosity is a way God brings increase to you. You can give your way out of debt. Your tithing and your giving will open up supernatural resources in your life. God said it to me like this, **"If you will get addicted to giving, I will support your habit!"**

I like the story about the man who told his wife he had worked hard all his life for his money. He saved and saved. He said to her, "I will be the first one to take my money with me when I die. As a matter of fact, all my money is in the attic. When I die, I am going to take it with me." After he died, his wife climbed up in the attic, and found all the money was still there! So she said, "Hmm, I guess he should have put it in the basement!" (Ha ha ha! So he could get it on the way down.) That is a funny story, but many people have wrong ideas about money.

Some say money is evil, but that is not true. Money itself is not evil. The Bible says the *LOVE* of money is the root of all evil (1 Timothy 6:10). **God is not opposed to us being rich; but He is opposed to us being covetous (Dad Hagin).** Covetousness is being stingy and constantly chasing money. Matthew 6:33 says, *"But seek ye first the kingdom of God, and his righteousness; and all these things shall be added unto you."*

We are to seek God, not money. And when we give and are generous we demonstrate that God is our source. Money is not our source. Our trust is in the living God.

66 You may not go *where no man* has ever gone before, but you can go where no one in *your family* has ever been before.

Mark Hankins

9

TITHING: THE PLACE TO START

The tithe is the first step to honoring God with your money. It is just the beginning of generosity. Malachi 3:8-12, instructs us to give our tithe, which is 10 percent of all our increase, to the house of God.

Some people want to tip God or put Him on salary with a set amount each week. The problem with that is if you put God on salary, then He works for you. However, if you give Him 10 percent (the tithe), you become His partner. And it is to His advantage to increase you because He knows you are going to turn around and sow the increase right back into His Kingdom. **My dad always told me, "You can**

tithe on what you make or on what you want to make."

Some people argue they do not have to tithe because it is an Old Testament law. Actually, Abraham was the first tither (Hebrews 7:1-7), and he lived before the law was ever given. Hebrews 7:8 says, *"And here men that die receive tithes; but there he receiveth them, of whom it is witnessed that he liveth."* In the new covenant, the tithe witnesses that Jesus is alive. Tithing is really just an act of faith, following in the steps of our Father Abraham (Romans 4:12).

I heard a story about a rich man who went to his pastor and said, "Pastor, I have tithed all my life and I have a lot of money now. In fact, I have so much money that I think I will just give a little something here and there. I cannot give 10 percent anymore." The pastor said, "That is fine, but let me pray with you before you leave." The pastor prayed this prayer, "Lord, I ask You to reduce my brother's income to the place where he will be able to tithe again." This is humorous, but so true. When you commit to be a tither, it is nonnegotiable. Ten percent of all the money that comes in to your hands belongs to the Lord.

Here is a list of some of the notable tithers in America you might recognize:

William Colgate, who founded the Colgate shaving cream and toothpaste company, started tithing when he was a young man. He then increased his giving to 20 percent, then to 30 percent, then to 40 percent, then to 50 percent. Eventually, he saved enough money to live on and gave God all of his income.

John D. Rockefeller was an American oil industry business industrialist and philanthropist. He began tithing at eight years old. He said, "I tithed on every dollar that God entrusted to me. I want to say to you that I could have never tithed on my first million if I had not tithed on my first salary of $1.50 a week." He is widely considered one of the wealthiest Americans of all time.

R.G. LeTourneau was a born-again believer and inventor of earthmoving machinery. He accepted Christ and decided to make God his business partner. Everything went well for a few years until he started to get behind financially. He told God, "I cannot afford to tithe. Just give me a chance to build the business and then I will tithe." LeTourneau realized his mistake after almost going bankrupt. He said he talked to God and God told him, "It takes faith to tithe on the front side and not wait and give what is left over." So LeTourneau made the adjustment and learned to give his first fruits to God and make this a lifestyle. He kept doing this until he became a very wealthy man in Heaven as well as on earth. He actually progressed in generosity to the point of giving 90 percent of his income and living on 10 percent.

I do not know about you, but I would rather have 10 percent of $10 million than 90 percent of $50,000. When you get in covenant or partnership with God, He can take you places in the blessing of the Lord you have never been before. **You may not go where no man has ever gone before, but you can go where no one in your family has ever been before.** God wants to take you to new levels of His blessing.

66 If you get
addicted
to giving-
God will
support
your habit.

Mark Hankins

10

OPEN A DEBIT AND CREDIT ACCOUNT

One of the characteristics that Paul noted about the church in Philippi was their generosity. Philippians 4:15,16 says, *"...no church communicated with me as concerning giving and receiving, but ye only. For even in Thessalonica ye sent once again unto my necessity."*

This church's generosity got Paul's attention! Another translation reads, *"...no church (assembly) entered into partnership with me and opened up [a debit and credit] account in giving and receiving except you only"* (Philippians 4:15 AMP). Not only was this church generous, they were continually generous. Their giving was not required by Paul. It came from their strong desire to meet the needs he had.

Paul was pleased and added in verse 17, *"Not because I desire a gift, but I desire fruit that may abound to your account."* This was not just about giving, but receiving also. That tells me there must be a heavenly bank account where you can make deposits and withdrawals.

David Baron, a Bible Scholar, saith that there is no limits to God's giving, except His creature's capacity to receive.

> *Oh how great is thy goodness, which thou hast laid up for them that fear thee; which thou hast wrought for them that trust in thee before the sons of men!*
> *-Psalm 31:19*

> *What a stack of blessing you have piled up for those who worship you.*
> *-Message*

When the Philippian church gave to Paul financially, it resulted in abundance and all their needs were fully supplied.

Paul said in verse 18, *"I am full, having received of Epaphroditus the things which were sent from you, an odour of a sweet smell, a sacrifice acceptable, well pleasing to God."* Something outstanding happened after Paul received the offerings. Their sacrifice got the attention of God. Though their giving was to Paul and his ministry, it was a sweet smelling sacrifice in Heaven.

Anytime you get God's attention by giving, get ready to receive something from Him. Get ready for the blessing!

Paul concluded by blessing his partners. Look at what he says in Philippians 4.

> *But my God shall supply all your need according to his riches in glory by Christ Jesus.*
> *-Philippians 4:19*

> *And my God, on the scale of his wealth, will fully supply in Christ Jesus your every need in [heaven's] glory.*
> *-Hudson*

And every need of yours my God will satisfy in Glory through Christ Jesus (as His inexhaustible resources enable Him to do).

-Wade

When you jump in the middle of a ministry's need, God jumps in the middle of your need!

66 If *your giving* doesn't affect you much, neither will *your harvest.*

Mark Hankins

11

HARVESTS NEVER GET CONFUSED

But this I say, He which soweth sparingly shall reap also sparingly; and he which soweth bountifully shall reap also bountifully.
-2 Corinthians 9:6

One time I asked the Lord about generosity, specifically about sowing bountifully. I wanted to have more understanding and revelation. I said, "Lord, You said that if I sow sparingly, I will reap sparingly and that if I sow generously, I will reap generously. I am interested in the generous harvest." The Lord said, **"Harvests never get confused."**

It is quite simple. You do not have to worry about sowing sparingly and reaping generously. Neither do you have to worry about sowing generously and reaping sparingly. When you sow your seed, it is automatically labeled sparing or generous, and it has your return address on it. Your harvest will come directly to you and nobody can block it.

The Lord also told me, **"If your giving does not affect you much, neither will your harvest."** I purposed in my heart right then to be generous. I asked the Lord, "How will I know when I am generous?" I was not sure because generous can be different amounts to different people. He said, "You will know, because when you are generous you will think about it for months and even years later!"

When you are generous, you get outside of your comfort zone. You are looking to Him alone and saying, "I know there is a God and my God is faithful: He cannot lie and He can be depended on!" You are believing and trusting God to watch over His Word to perform it!

66 The seed is *guaranteed*. It has a *return address.* Your harvest *never gets confused!*

Mark Hankins

12

FARMING MONEY

Poor sowing means a poor harvest, and generous
sowing means a generous harvest.
-2 Corinthians 9:6 (Phillips)

A pastor once told me, "Sowing is not necessary."
I thought, "Tell that to a farmer!" Farmers will borrow
money to buy seed. Seedtime and harvest are actually
God's idea. Genesis 1:12 says, *"And the earth brought forth*
grass, and herb yielding seed after his kind, and the tree yielding
fruit, whose seed was in itself, after his kind: and God saw that
it was good. Seedtime and harvest still works the same as it did

in the beginning." And they will never cease as long as the earth remains according to Genesis 8:22. God has designed the whole program.

KEEP YOUR PLANTER WORKING

I visited with a farmer in eastern Colorado who asked me which piece of farm machinery I thought was most valuable. I guessed different things and was surprised to hear his answer, but it made sense. The most important implement a farmer uses is called the planter. This is the machine that puts the seed in the ground. A farmer will actually borrow thousands of dollars to keep it working. If there is a bare spot in the field at harvest time, the first place the farmer will check is the planter to see if it needs repair. If there is no seed in the ground, there will be no crop, no harvest, and no increase. If I am experiencing lack, the first thing I check is my sowing.

SOWING IS NOT THROWING

A farmer does not just drive down the road throwing seed out on the ground and hoping it will grow. No! He sows strategically and systematically, with the exact same distance between seeds. He sows his seed in prepared soil, expecting a harvest. Likewise, we must sow in expectation. Ecclesiastes 11:1 says, *"Cast thy bread upon the waters: for thou shalt find it after many days."* The Lord told me, "It is the *many days* that scare people." But you can have a confident expectation that there will be a harvest on your seed sown!

SOAK YOUR SEED

There are some seeds that are soaked in water or fertilizer for a time before they are planted. When you soak the seeds before planting, you greatly decrease the amount of time it takes for the seeds to germinate. The water causes the hard, protective exterior to soften and the germination to speed up. Whatever you plant will grow more quickly and produce a better harvest.

You may have heard the phrase, "Money does not grow on trees." It will if you plant it! When you take scriptures concerning finances, meditate on them, and thank God for His promises, you are soaking that financial seed you are about to plant. Maybe your seed is already in the ground. Speak the Word, soak it, and watch it grow!

KNOW WHERE AND WHEN TO SOW

Where should you plant your seed? What is the best ground for getting the greatest yield? Sow your financial seed—your money—in response to the Word of God you have received. Sow into the church or ministries where you have been taught the Word of God. Sow in response to God's Word and to the degree that Word has ministered to you.

SOW WITH A HARVEST IN MIND

Once you see the power of the seed, you then purpose in your heart to give. And you give not always to meet a ministry's need, but sometimes because you need a harvest. As you sow consistently there will never be a season where you are unproductive financially. You will have a harvest!

66 Over and above *giving* produces over and above *living*.

Mark Hankins

13

A WHOPPER OF
A HARVEST

Brother Kenneth Copeland is someone I look up to in the faith. I have been a monthly partner with him for many years. The Lord told him years ago, "I am going to teach you how to get rich through giving."

For his 80th birthday party, I was asked to emcee the program because they wanted me to tell a few jokes. They did not want the party to be too serious.

Of course, I wanted to take a significant and generous offering to the party with me. Brother Copeland has been such a blessing to our lives and this generation, and generosity is connected to honor. **You show respect with words, but you honor**

with substance. Honor will always cost you something, but will always bring great reward.

Now, Trina and I had just returned from ministering in 12 nations in 12 months. We were exhausted, and as soon as I got home, my secretary said, "We are behind $150,000 in bills right now." Despite the financial challenges I was facing, I told her to write a check to Brother Copeland. I chose to honor him with a generous offering.

At the party, Brother Copeland's best partners and preacher friends were all there. I told a few jokes and stories and gave my special offering. We all had a wonderful time celebrating his birthday.

A few days later, I was preaching in Bogotà, Colombia, when I got a phone call from Brother Copeland. He said, "Mark, I am sitting on my back porch looking at the lake. I appreciate you being at my party. I have been laughing every day about your funny stories and jokes. I have this offering you gave. That is a whopper of a seed. I want to tell you that you are going to get a **WHOPPER OF A HARVEST**." I said, "Yes, sir. I am expecting a whopper of a harvest." When we hung up, I jumped all over the room rejoicing and saying, "I have got a whopper of a harvest coming!"

Do you know God guarantees to multiply your seed sown? It was not even a few weeks later and we had a whopper of a harvest come in for the ministry. Praise God!

Sometimes when you are sowing, the devil will tell you, "What are you going to do if that does not work?" I like to turn it around and say, "Devil, what are you going to do when it does work?" Do not let the devil scare you out of generosity. When the devil tries to scare you or circumstances seem to limit you, remember that your generosity will take you beyond your talent and circumstances. God will make all grace abound to you.

God said it to me this way: "God's kingdom sowing system will always outperform the world's savings system." There is nothing wrong with saving. I believe in saving. God just said, "Your sowing will outperform your savings."

It is a step of spiritual growth to receive God's generosity and then say, "Lord, let me be generous in my generation. I want to be generous toward the preaching of the Gospel of Christ, which is the number one need of the world. Let me be generous to the church, which is the number one need of America." Even after your funeral, I promise your generosity will still be speaking.

66 The *Word works* for you when you get *thrilled* with it!

Dad Hagin

14

MEDITATION: HOW TO TAP INTO HEAVEN'S SUPPLY

I rejoice at thy word, as one that findeth great spoil.
-Psalm 119:162

I'm ecstatic over what you say, like one who strikes it rich.
-Message

In addition to sowing your seed, you must take time to meditate in God's Word. Many times this is the step between sowing and reaping. Let me illustrate what I mean.

Years ago, I went to eat with some friends at a Japanese restaurant. They were eating sushi and showed me some green stuff called wasabi. They warned me to be careful with it because it was very hot. I had never tried wasabi, but I am from Texas, where we eat jalapeno peppers. I was not scared of that small green substance. I picked up a big bite of sushi and told them to give me extra wasabi. I dipped my sushi in it and put the whole thing in my mouth. All of a sudden, *BOOM*! In less than three seconds, that wasabi hit me in the head and I felt like my brain was going to explode! It was a very unusual experience. WASABI!

Later, I was meditating on the Word of God and just thinking God's thoughts. God's Word is full of His thoughts. See, He does not think like humans do. His thoughts and ways are higher than ours (Isaiah 55:8-9). The more we meditate on His thoughts, the more they will saturate our whole being and we'll begin to learn how He thinks.

While I was meditating on the Word concerning generosity, I felt the living Word of God come up on the inside of me, challenge my thinking, and hit me in the brain. I thought, "WASABI!"

The Word of God is alive and full of power. Sometimes just a couple of God's thoughts will totally overwhelm you, just like that wasabi! This is true in the realm of generosity.

Let's look at meditation more closely. Remember, one of the ways God has provided for believers to think His thoughts is through meditation in His Word. I like what Norman Vincent Peale said, **"It is almost as if there were an invisible reservoir in the universe that can be tapped if you will just obey certain spiritual laws."**

In difficult times people search out a variety of resources to sustain themselves. But those who put their trust in God and learn to tap into His supply will not lack. They will even flourish! But the art of meditation on God's Word draws out His wisdom and His supernatural power to produce amazing results.

Meditation is often overlooked and skipped as we go through the daily affairs of life. That is why it is important to study how to meditate and what to meditate on, especially if you want to see results. Let's look at some scriptures regarding meditation.

But his delight is in the law of the Lord; and in His law doth he meditate day and night; and He shall be like a tree that's planted by the rivers of water, that bringeth forth his fruit in his season; his leaf also shall not wither and whatsoever he doeth shall prosper.

-Psalm 1:2-3

You thrill to God's Word, you chew on Scripture day and night. You're a tree replanted in Eden, bearing fresh fruit every month, never dropping a leaf, always in blossom.

-Message

Most blessed is the man who believes in, trusts in, and relies on the Lord, and whose hope and confidence the Lord is. For he shall be like a tree planted by the waters that spreads out its roots by the river; and it shall not see and fear when heat comes; but its leaf shall be green, It

*shall not be anxious and full of care in the year
of drought, nor shall it cease yielding fruit.*
-Jeremiah 17:7,8 (AMP)

*He is like a tree planted along the riverbank,
with its roots reaching deep into the water—a
tree not bothered by the heat nor worried by long
months of drought. Its leaves stay green...*
-The Living Bible

*Most blessed is the man who trusts me, God,
the woman who sticks with God. They're
like trees replanted in Eden, putting down
roots near the rivers. Never a worry through
the hottest of summers, never dropping a leaf,
serene and calm through droughts, bearing
fresh fruit every season.*
-Message

*He is like a tree by the water side that thrusts
its roots to the stream: when the heat comes it
feels no alarm, its foliage stays green; it has no*

worries in the year of drought, and never ceases
to bear fruit.
-Jerusalem

Meditation bring success (Joshua 1:8)! In 1 Timothy 4:15, Paul said, *"meditate upon these things; give thyself wholly to them, that thy profiting may appear to all."* When a tree is well watered, it is evident to all. You can see the fruit and the green leaves. In the same way, those around you can see the results of the Word working in your life—the result of your meditation. The fruit of blessing is very tangible!

HOW TO MEDITATE

To meditate means to talk with yourself, mutter, or cogitate. It is an inward and outward conversation. It means to study, chew over, think over, ponder, excogitate, muse, reflect, mull over, and speculate. The word "cogitate" means to think deeply, think out, think up, dream up, and to hatch. Excogitate is to invent or create mentally. Christian meditation is NOT sitting on the floor with your legs crossed, humming to yourself, and emptying your mind. Meditation is a relationship with the Word of God.

If you know how to worry or if you have been offended, then you know how to meditate. You constantly think about what could happen, or what is happening and speculate about the results. And those thoughts even affect your body and emotions!

Philippians 4:6,7 tells us not to worry about anything, but to turn those worries into requests followed by thanksgiving. God promises to surround our hearts with His peace. Verse 8 goes on to tell us that our part is to do something with our thoughts. We are to meditate, or think about, things that are true, honest, just, pure, lovely, virtuous, and of good report. We are to begin praising instead of worrying.

Through meditation, the Word becomes engrafted in you and is able to save, or restore, your soul, which is your mind, will, and emotions (James 1:21). When you are speaking the Word of God— pondering it, muttering it, turning it over, digesting it, and dreaming about all of those great promises given to you—something happens. You begin to draw up divine power, just like a tree draws water out of the soil it is planted in.

FEAST ON THE WORD

*Your words were found and I did eat them and
they were to me the joy and rejoicing of my heart.
-Jeremiah 15:16*

*When your words showed up, I ate them—
swallowed them whole. What a feast!
-Message*

*When your words came, I devoured them.
-Jerusalem*

*Your words are what sustained me, they are
food to my soul.
-The Living Bible*

My mother was the slowest eater I have ever
known! We would start our meal together and two
hours later she would still be chewing! I would tell
her to take the rest home because I had things to do!
She would then tell me the benefits of eating slowly.
Doctors say you should chew your food 32 times before

swallowing and that digestion begins in your mouth where the food is broken down before you swallow.

God's Word is the same way. It is faith food, and it is meant to be chewed—to be eaten. Matthew 4:4 says, *"Man shall not live by bread alone, but by every word that proceedeth out of the mouth of God."* Faith comes by hearing and hearing by the Word of God (Romans 10:17). But that Word has to be digested for faith to come. When you meditate, the Word does exactly that. It gets in your eyes, your ears, your mouth, and then into your entire body.

GET RESULTS

In Mark 4, Jesus taught the importance of hearing the Word and compared it to a seed. The most important thing was for the roots of the seed to go down into the soil, causing growth and eventually fruit to come forth.

Wherever there is a need in your life, begin to gather seeds of the Word. Then you can plant them in your heart and grow a crop of healing, peace, finances, your family's salvation—whatever it is you need. In 1

Corinthians 3:6 it says, *"I have planted, Apollos watered; but God gave the increase."* The planting occurs when you first hear the Word. But it must be watered by repetition. Some reject the watering process and get no results from the Word they heard. If you have seen no increase, now is the time to check out your watering, or your meditation, of the Word.

DELIGHT IN THE LAW OF THE LORD

David said his delight was in the law of the Lord. What are those laws? They are God's Word. They are the Law of Faith (Romans 3:27); the Law of Love (1 Corinthians 13); the Law of the Spirit of Life (Romans 8:2), and of course the Law of Sowing and Reaping (2 Corinthians 9:6-11). Every Christian is personally responsible to tap into the power of God in these areas if they want to live above the corruption in the world.

Psalm 119, the longest chapter in the Bible, overflows with David's love for God's Word. He mentions meditation seven times. The psalms he sang were, in fact, a form of meditation. In Psalm 104:33,34

He said, *"I will sing unto the Lord as long as I live: I will sing praise to my God while I have my being. My meditation of him shall be sweet: I will be glad in the Lord."* What a great example for us to follow.

TAP INTO ABUNDANCE

As you meditate on God's Word it will begin to flood your consciousness. It will walk off the page and into your heart, living and abiding in you. It will guide you into good success every step of the way, every night and day. You will have tapped into that great reservoir of abundance! You will have the mind of Christ. You will enter the realm where all things are possible.

> *Knowing that whatsoever good thing any man doeth, the same shall he receive of the Lord, whether he be bond or free.*
> *-Ephesians 6:8*

> *I rejoice at thy word, as one that findeth great spoil.*
> *-Psalm 119:162*

I'm ecstatic over what you say, like one who
strikes it rich.
-Psalm 119:162 (Message)

Whatever part of the Bible you get thrilled about is what will work for you. The simplest definition of faith is to act like the Bible is true. When it comes to generosity, as you apply the principles of gving and receiving you will experience God's abundant provision.

CONFESSIONS TO BOLDY DECLARE

God is on my side
For the Blood has been applied,
Every need shall be supplied,
Nothing shall be denied.
So I enter into rest
I know that I am Blessed.
I have passed the test.
I will get God's best!
Trina Hankins

The Lord is my Shepherd I shall not want. I do not lack for ability, I do not lack for opportunity, and I never lack for money (Psalm 23:1)!

My God shall supply all of my needs according to His riches in Glory by Christ Jesus (Philippians 4:19)!

My Father God always takes care of me in grand style! God never fails to plan the best things for His children (Mark 11:23).

Personal Notes

Personal Notes

Personal Notes

Personal Notes

Personal Notes

References

Amplified Bible. Zondervan Publishing House, Grand Rapids, Michigan, 1972.

Barron, D. (1918). *Zechariah: A Commentary on His Visions and Prophecies.* London: Kreigel Publications.

Godbey, W.B. *Translation of the New Testament.* Newby Bookroom, Indiana, 1973.

Hudson, J, (1958). *The Pauline Epistles, Their Meaning and Message.* London: James Clarke and Co., Ltd.

Jerusalem Bible. Double Day and Company, Inc., New York, New York, 1968.

LeTournea, R. (1960). *R.G. LeTourneau: Mover of Men and Mountains.* Chicago, IL: Moody Publishers.

Moffat, J. *The Holy Bible Containing the Old and New Testaments.* Double Day and Company, Inc., New York, New York, 1926.

New English Bible. Oxford University Press, Oxford, England, 1961.

New Living Translation. Tyndale House Publishers. Wheaton, Ill: 1996.

Peale, N. (1952). *The Power of Positive Thinking.* New York, NY: Prentice-Hall Inc.

Peterson, Eugene. *The Message//Remix, The Bible in Contemporary Language.* NavPress Publishing Group, Colorado Springs, Colorado, 2003.

Phillips, J.B. *The New Testament in Modern English.* The MacMillan Company, New York, New York, 1958.

Taylor, Ken. *The Living Bible.* Tyndale House Publishers, Wheaton, Illinois, 1971.

Wade, G.W. *The Documents of the New Testament.* Thomas Burby and Company, London, England, 1934.

Acknowledgments

Special Thanks to my wife, Trina.

My son, Aaron and his wife, Errin Cody; their daughters, Avery Jane and Macy Claire, their son, Jude Aaron.

My daughter, Alicia and her husband, Caleb; their sons, Jaiden Mark, Gavin Luke, Landon James, and Dylan Paul, their daughter Hadley Marie.

My parents, Pastor B.B. and Velma Hankins, who are now in Heaven with the Lord.

My wife's parents, Rev. William and Ginger Behrman.

About the Authors

Mark and Trina Hankins travel nationally and internationally preaching the Word of God with the power of the Holy Spirit. Their message centers on the spirit of faith, who the believer is in Christ, and the work of the Holy Spirit.

After over forty years of pastoral and traveling ministry, Mark and Trina are now ministering full-time in campmeetings, leadership conferences, and church services around the world and across the United States. Their son, Aaron, and his wife Errin Cody, are now the pastors of Christian Worship Center in Alexandria, Louisiana. Their daughter, Alicia Moran, and her husband Caleb, pastor Metro Life Church in Lafayette, Louisiana. Mark and Trina have eight grandchildren.

Mark and Trina have written several books. For more information on Mark Hankins Ministries, log on to our website, www.markhankins.org.

CONNECT WITH US

P.O. BOX 12863 ALEXANDRIA, LA 71315 ‖ 318.767.2001

 MARKHANKINSMINISTRIES1123

 MARKHANKINS1123

 MARKHANKINS1123

 MARK HANKINS MINISTRIES TV

 WWW.MARKHANKINS.ORG

 MARK HANKINS MINISTRIES

 MARK HANKINS MINISTRIES

Mark Hankins Ministries Publications

SPIRIT-FILLED SCRIPTURE STUDY GUIDE
A comprehensive study of scriptures in over 120 different translations on topics such as: Redemption, Faith, Finances, Prayer and many more.

THE BLOODLINE OF A CHAMPION - THE POWER OF THE BLOOD OF JESUS
The blood of Jesus is the liquid language of love that flows from the heart of God and gives us hope in all circumstances. In this book, you will clearly see what the blood has done FOR US but also what the blood has done IN US as believers.

TAKING YOUR PLACE IN CHRIST
Many Christians talk about what they are trying to be and what they are going to be. This book is about who you are NOW as believers in Christ.

PAUL'S SYSTEM OF TRUTH

Paul's System of Truth reveals man's redemption in Christ, the reality of what happened from the cross to the throne and how it is applied for victory in life through Jesus Christ.

THE SECRET POWER OF JOY

If you only knew what happens in the Spirit when you rejoice, you would rejoice everyday. Joy is one of the great secrets of faith. This book will show you the importance of the joy of the Lord in a believer's life.

11:23 – THE LANGUAGE OF FAITH

Never under-estimate the power of one voice. Over 100 inspirational, mountain-moving quotes to "stir up" the spirit of faith in you.

LET THE GOOD TIMES ROLL

This book focuses on the five key factors to heaven on earth: The Holy Spirit, Glory, Faith, Joy, and Redemption. The Holy Spirit is a genius. If you will listen to Him, He will make you look smart.

THE POWER OF IDENTIFICATION WITH CHRIST

Learn how God identified us with Christ in His death, burial, resurrection, and seating in Heaven. The same identical life, victory, joy, and blessings that are In Christ are now in you. This is the glory and the mystery of Christianity – the power of the believer's identification with Christ.

REVOLUTIONARY REVELATION

This book provides excellent insight on how the spirit of wisdom and revelation is mandatory for believers to access their call, inheritance, and authority in Christ.

FAITH OPENS THE DOOR TO THE SUPERNATURAL

In this book you will learn how believing and speaking open the door to the supernatural.

DIVINE APPROVAL

Understanding you have God's divine approval on your life sets your free from the sense of rejection or inferiority. This confidence in God sets you free from constantly seeking approval from others.

NEVER RUN AT YOUR GIANT WITH YOUR MOUTH SHUT

We all face many giants in life that must be conquered before we can receive and do all that God has for us. Winning the War of words is necessary to win the fight of faith. So...Lift your voice!

THE SPIRIT OF FAITH

If you only knew what was on the other side of your mountain, you would move it! Having a spirit of faith is necessary to do the will of God and fulfill your destiny.

GOD'S HEALING WORD by Trina Hankins

Trina's testimony and a practical guide to receiving healing through meditating on the Word of God. This guide includes: testimonies, practical teaching, Scriptures & confessions, and a CD with Scriptures & confessions (read by Mark Hankins).

Mark Hankins Ministries

PO BOX 12863 ALEXANDRIA, LA 71315
Phone: 318.767.2001 E-mail: contact@markhankins.org
Visit us on the web: www.markhankins.org